TODAY I AM MAD

by Michael Gordon

Go https://michaelgordonclub.wixsite.com/books **to get** "The Grumpy Dinosaur" for **FREE!**

THIS BOOK BELONGS TO

....

....

At playschool, Josh was hunting for his favorite toy.
But the engine that he wanted was with another boy.

Upset, Josh didn't want this problem to spoil his whole day.
He didn't want to share with Tom; he wanted his own way.

As Josh watched Tom play with the toy, he started to feel worse. The other boy was having fun and Josh felt envious.

He rushed over to his classmate and grabbed away the toy.
"That's my favorite engine!" Josh yelled, then felt a rush of joy.

But his joy turned to regret when he saw that Tom looked sad.
Though Josh wanted the engine, he didn't want Tom to feel bad.

Josh was a good boy at heart, so he knew just what to do.
He said to Tom, "I'm sorry. I shouldn't have been mean you."

Tom smiled and forgave him. "It's a great engine, I like it too."
Josh nodded in agreement. "Maybe I can play with you?"

"I'd really like that," Tom said. "We can share, it will be fun."
Josh felt proud that he'd said sorry. A new friendship had begun.

That evening, while dinner cooked, Josh said he couldn't wait.
He grabbed a chocolate cookie from the pile on a plate.

Mom saw him and she shook her head; she took the treat away.
"Dinner will be ready soon, Josh. Go outside and play."

Josh huffed and puffed in anger and stomped off to the yard.
He knew he had to calm himself, but sometimes that was hard.

He breathed deeply in and out like Mama said he should.
He counted slowly one to ten and started to feel good.

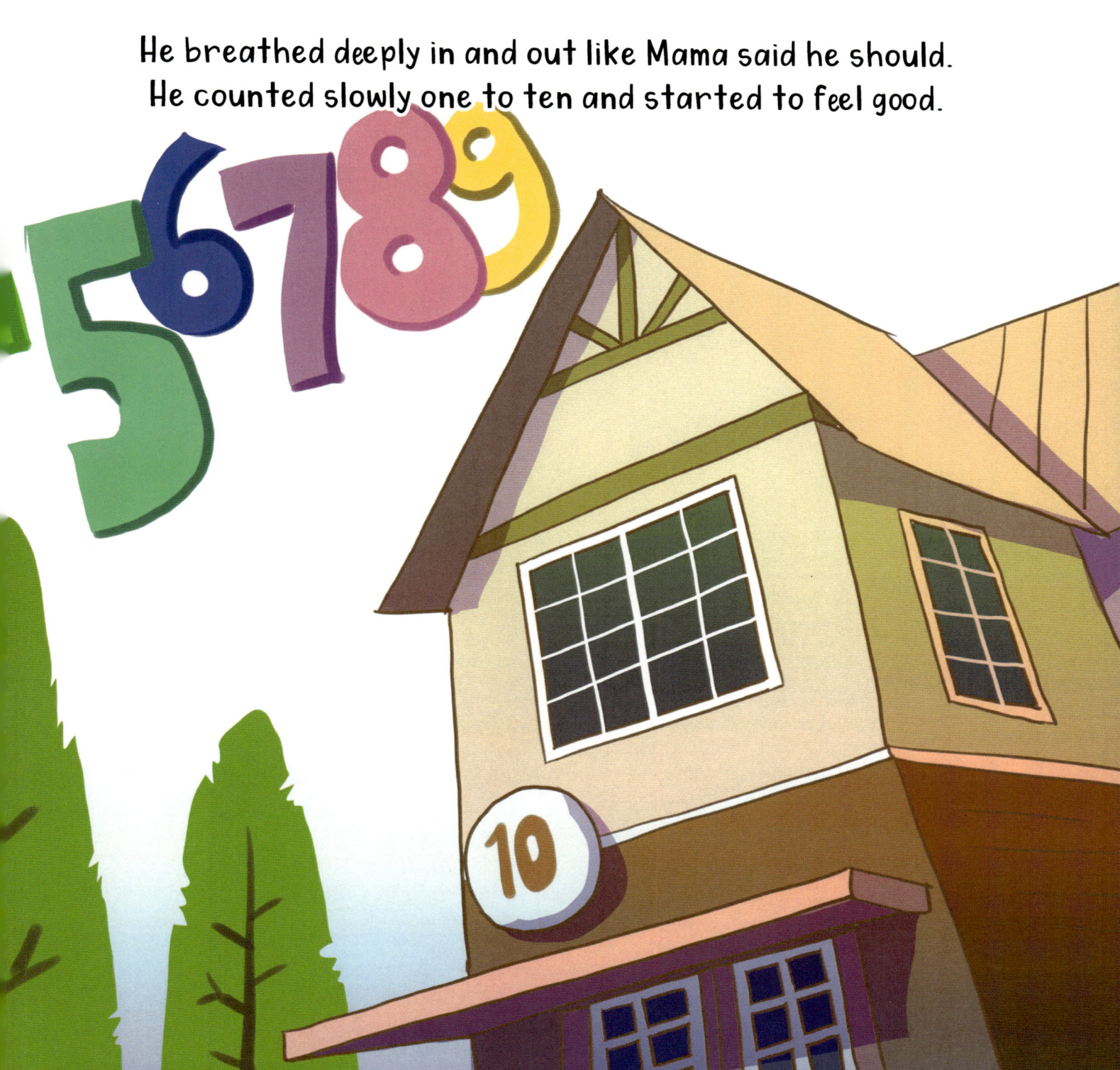

Feeling angry makes it hard to feel happy and swell.
Josh kicked a ball around the yard, knowing he'd done well.

He'd learned to let go of the things that had him feeling mad.
He'd managed his emotions well; he felt so proud and glad.

That night, while Josh was waiting for his story to be read,
His dad came into the room and sat down on the bed.

Dad smiled and hugged his son real tight as he began to say,
"I'm so proud of how you managed your emotions today."

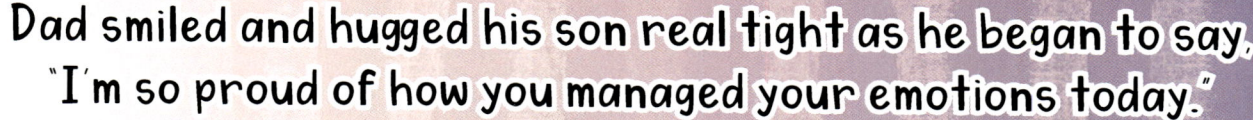

Two classmates were arguing at school the following day,
About which game would be the best for both of them to play.

George shouted and then, in a huff, he stomped off out the door.
Jordan cried and threw the game, then slumped down to the floor.

When Josh was upset, he loved to get hugs from Mom and Dad.
A hug is a good thing to give when people are feeling sad.

Josh wanted to make his friend feel better the best way he could.
He hugged Jordan tightly until he started to feel good.

About author

Michael Gordon is the talented author of several highly rated children's books including the popular Sleep Tight, Little Monster, and the Animal Bedtime.

He collaborates with the renowned Kids Book Book that creates picture books for all of ages to enjoy. Michael's goal is to create books that are engaging, funny, and inspirational for children of all ages and their parents.

Contact

For all other questions about books or author, please e-mail michaelgordonclub@gmail.com.

Thank You!
For purchasing this book,
I'd like to give you a free gift
An amazing bedtime story for your child
https://michaelgordonclub.wixsite.com/books

© 2019 Michael Gordon. All rights reserved.

All rights reserved. This book or parts thereof may not be reproduced in any form, stored in any retrieval system, or transmitted in any form by any means—electronic, mechanical, photocopy, recording, or otherwise—without prior written permission of the publisher, except as provided by United States of America copyright law

Go https://michaelgordonclub.wixsite.com/books **to get** "The Grumpy Dinosaur" for **FREE!**

Made in the USA
Columbia, SC
07 November 2019